Mel Bay Presents

QUARTAL HARMONY
& Voicings for Guitar

by Tom Floyd

Online Audio

To Access the Online Audio Go To:
www.melbay.com/99971MEB

Visit us on the Web at www.melbay.com — E-mail us at email@melbay.com

ONLINE AUDIO

1	Example 1, page 13 [0:24]*	31	Example 3, page 29 [0:10]	61	Example 2, page 49 [0:13]
2	Example 2, page 13 [0:25]*	32	Example 1, page 30 [0:16]*	62	Example 3, page 50 [0:14]
3	Example 3, page 13 [0:29]*	33	Example 2, page 31 [0:12]	63	Example 4, page 50 [0:13]
4	Example 4, page 14 [0:30]*	34	Example 3, page 31 [0:09]	64	Example 5, page 50 [0:12]
5	Example 5, page 14 [0:15]	35	Example 1, page 32 [0:19]*	65	Example 1, page 52 [0:09]
6	Example 6, page 15 [0:22]	36	Example 2, page 33 [0:12]	66	Example 2, page 52 [0:09]
7	Example 7, page 16 [0:14]	37	Example 3, page 33 [0:07]	67	Example 3, page 52 [0:10]
8	Example 1, page 17 [0:23]*	38	Example 1, page 34 [0:19]*	68	Example 4, page 52 [0:08]
9	Example 2, page 17 [0:24]*	39	Example 2, page 35 [0:10]	69	Example 5, page 53 [0:08]
10	Example 3, page 18 [0:23]*	40	Example 3, page 35 [0:07]	70	Example 6, page 53 [0:09]
11	Example 4, page 18 [0:15]	41	Example 1, page 38 [0:16]*	71	Example 7, page 53 [0:11]
12	Example 5, page 18 [0:13]	42	Example 2, page 38 [0:13]	72	Example 8, page 53 [0:10]
13	Example 1, page 19 [0:09]	43	Example 3, page 39 [0:07]	73	Example 9, page 53 [0:09]*
14	Example 2, page 19 [0:08]	44	Example 4, page 39 [0:10]	74	Example 10, page 53 [0:10]*
15	Example 3, page 19 [0:08]	45	Example 5, page 40 [0:11]	75	Example 11, page 54 [0:10]*
16	Example 4, page 20 [0:08]	46	Example 6, page 40 [0:11]	76	Example 12, page 54 [0:10]*
17	Example 5, page 20 [0:07]	47	Example 1, page 42 [0:12]	77	Example 13, page 54 [0:12]*
18	Example 6, page 20 [0:08]	48	Example 2, page 42 [0:09]	78	Example 14, page 54 [0:10]*
19	Example 7, page 21 [0:09]	49	Example 3, page 42 [0:12]	79	Example 15, page 54 [0:10]*
20	Example 1, page 23 [0:18]*	50	Example 4, page 43 [0:12]	80	Example 16, page 54 [0:10]*
21	Example 2, page 23 [0:10]	51	Example 5, page 43 [0:11]*	81	Example 17, page 55 [0:11]*
22	Example 3, page 23 [0:09]	52	Example 1, page 44 [0:17]	82	Example 18, page 55 [0:11]*
23	Example 1, page 24 [0:16]*	53	Example 2, page 45 [0:14]	83	Example 19, page 55 [0:11]*
24	Example 2, page 25 [0:11]	54	Example 3, page 45 [0:09]	84	"Minor Blues", pg. 63 [0:27]*
25	Example 3, page 25 [0:08]	55	Example 4, page 46 [0:08]	85	"500 Chicks", pg. 65 [0:48]
26	Example 1, page 26 [0:10]	56	Example 5, page 46 [0:15]	86	"Hand Prints", pg. 66 [0:45]
27	Example 2, page 27 [0:11]	57	Example 1, page 47 [0:14]	87	"Black in Grey", pg. 67 [0:37]
28	Example 3, page 27 [0:10]	58	Example 2, page 48 [0:12]	88	"Never Tardy", pg. 68 [0:53]
29	Example 1, page 28 [0:16]*	59	Example 3, page 48 [0:13]	89	"Big Moon Flower", pg. 69 [1:34]
30	Example 2, page 29 [0:10]	60	Example 1, page 49 [0:13]		

* (w/r.s.) = with rhythm section

TABLE OF CONTENTS

INTRODUCTION

Charlie Parker played his music in what was called the "Bop Era". "Bop" or "be-bop" refers to the jazz style that began in the 1940's. All of Parker's solo lines form the basis for practically the entire "be-bop" vocabulary. Many modern players still use Parker's musical phrases today, even in "outside" playing.

In the 60's there was a new direction in jazz. Miles Davis pioneered what was known as "The Birth Of The Cool". In this period John Coltrane emmerged with "Giant Steps". The compositions by Miles Davis and John Coltrane had chord progressions different than most jazz standards.

When we talk about Coltrane, we must remember that Coltrane built upon Parker's foundation. Coltrane used both his "cycle" and Parker's "cycle" in his improvisational vocabulary. Unlike Parker, Coltrane had the advantage of pianists Bill Evans and McCoy Tyner. Both had classical backgrounds and understood Parker's concepts. When Evans and Tyner joined with Coltrane, they understood his new "cycle" and added the use of quartal harmony to Coltrane's compositions. The foundation of "modern quartal harmony" began in this era.

The new "quartal concepts" caught on with all pianists involved with the new direction of jazz. Guitarists now had to delve into an area that was generated primarily by pianists.

Chord voicings using quartal harmony have been used for many years in jazz. Johnny Smith, Tal Farlow, Chuck Wayne, Barney Kessel, Joe Pass, Jimmy Raney, Wes Montgomery and other legendary guitarists used chords containing 4th harmony. They used 4th voicings in a traditional fashion, that is, as major 9th, 13th and minor 11th chords.

One of the first examples on guitar, using modern chordal harmony concepts, was by Jim Hall. The album *The Bridge*, by Sonny Rollins, showcased Jim Hall's use of quartal voicings.

The use of quartal harmony started to emerge in other guitarists, especially in the New York area. George Benson, Pat Martino, Jack Wilkins, and Joe Diorio were some of the most influential.

The first recordings that made a major impact on my interest in quartal harmony were by George Benson and Jack Wilkins.

George Benson's live version of "Skydive" and Jack Wilkins' version of "Windows" are, in my opinion, examples of major evolution of the guitar in the area of quartal harmony.

In other parts of the country, Howard Roberts, Kenny Burell and Wes Montgomery used modern quartal harmony concepts in tunes such as "Impressions," "So What" and "Little Sunflower."

There are currently many great guitarists that carry on the tradition of the great be-bop jazz musicians. In addition to be-bop concepts of harmony, quartal concepts have become a major part of mainstream jazz.

Some of the current leading guitarists using quartal concepts are: Henry Johnson, Russel Malone, Jimmy Bruno, Howard Alden, Paul Bollenback, Mark Whitfield, and Rodney Jones, in addition to the legendary Pat Martino, Jack Wilkins and George Benson.

In the early to mid 1970's jazz guitar fused with rock guitar, "jazz fusion" and "rock jazz fusion" were born. Some of the leading names were John McLaughlin, Pat Metheny, Larry Coryell and Al Dimeola. These guitarists were influenced by the main guitarists of the 1960's and were heavily influenced by John Coltrane and Miles Davis.

More rock-influenced guitarists in the 1980's began playing jazz. They were all influenced by their predecessors in the 1960's and 1970's. Compositions by John Coltrane and Miles Davis, using quartal harmony, became a main part of their repertoire.

At the present time, some of the most prominent jazz fusion guitarists are John Scofield, Alan Holdsworth, Scott Henderson, Robben Ford, Mike Stern and Frank Gambale.

You may want to acquire recordings, books, and videos by all of the guitarists mentioned above. Most music stores have catalogs and computer listings of available materials.

I hope that you find this book helpful in understanding "quartal harmony."

~ Tom Floyd ~

ABOUT THE AUTHOR

Tom Floyd has studied with many top guitarists and teachers including: Chuck Wayne, Sal Salvador, Don Arnone, Pat Martino, Sal LaPorta, Steve Watson and Vincent Bredice. He is presently the Jazz Guitar instructor at Florida Atlantic University.

TRADITIONAL HARMONY

- In traditional harmony, chords are formed by stacking notes in intervals of 3rds on each tone of the scale.

- The major and harmonic minor scale form the foundation for most traditional harmony.

- Building harmony in 3rds can also be applied to any other type of scale, such as, modes, diminished, whole-tone, melodic minor, etc.

C Major Harmonized Scale:

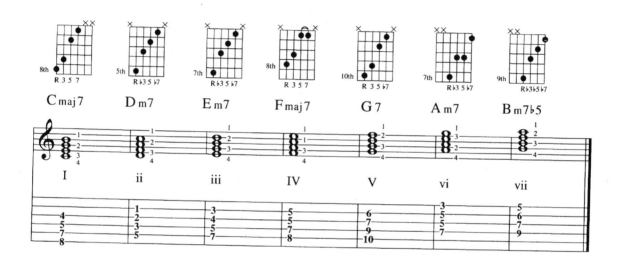

- The four notes contained in the **7th chord** are: the **root**, the **3rd**, the **5th**, and the **7th**.

- Chords may be played starting with the 3rd, 5th, or 7th instead of the root as the lowest sound, creating **inversions**.

- When you **harmonize** any major scale, in diatonic (whole-steps, ½ steps etc.– scales) 3rds you always wind up with the **same sequence** of chords.

I	ii	iii	IV	V	vi	vii
maj7	m7	m7	maj7	7th	m7	m7♭5

The Roman Numeral System

- CAPITAL Roman numerals identify **major chord types**: I-maj7, IV-maj7, and V-7th.

- SMALL Roman numerals identify **minor chord types**: ii-m7, iii-m7, vi-m7, and vii-m7b5

- The terminology **ii - V - I** in the key of C Major would mean: **Dm7 - G7 - Cmaj7**.

QUARTAL HARMONY

- Quartal harmony is constructed in the same fashion as traditional harmony, except 4th intervals are used instead of 3rds.

- Harmonizing a scale in 4ths is what is refered to as **quartal harmony**.

The Key of C Major in Quartal Harmony:

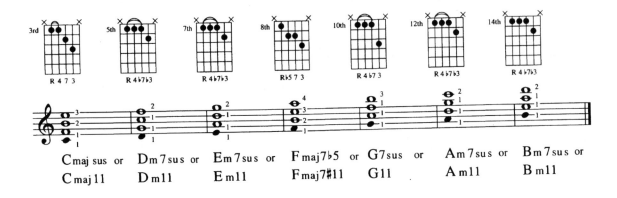

Cmaj sus or	Dm7sus or	Em7sus or	Fmaj7♭5 or	G7sus or	Am7sus or	Bm7sus or
Cmaj11	Dm11	Em11	Fmaj7♯11	G11	Am11	Bm11

FUNCTIONS

- The main difference between **traditional** and **quartal** harmony is the concept of "**functions**."

- The quartal chord forms can be used in the traditional fashion with the names Em7, Dm11 etc.

- Quartal harmonies can also be viewed as scale degree functions.

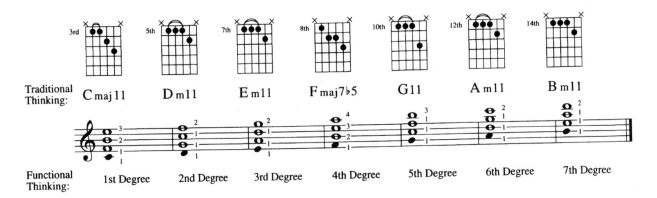

Traditional Thinking: Cmaj11   Dm11   Em11   Fmaj7♭5   G11   Am11   Bm11

Functional Thinking: 1st Degree   2nd Degree   3rd Degree   4th Degree   5th Degree   6th Degree   7th Degree

Example: Key of C

- **From C** - **C** (1st degree) **D** (2nd degree) **E** (3rd degree) etc.

- **From D** - **D** (1st degree) **E** (2nd degree) **F** (3rd degree) etc.

6

Quartal Situations:

- In many **jazz** and **fusion** tunes, one chord may be played for many measures.

- The example above has a key signature of all naturals (C major).

- We can assume that the Dm7 chord is the iim7 of C major.

- All of the quartal structures built in the key of C major, can function as harmonies to be played over Dm or a Dm bass line.

- This kind of thinking is also referred to as modal or in this case **Dorian**.

- In order to be able to play in this style we have to first learn the 4th structures on all three string groups.

UPPER, MIDDLE AND LOWER FOUR-STRING VOICINGS

Four-Note Voicings on the Upper Four Strings:

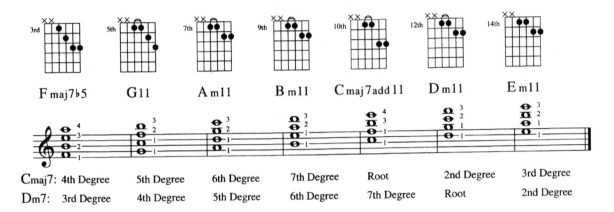

Four-Note Voicings on the Middle Four Strings:

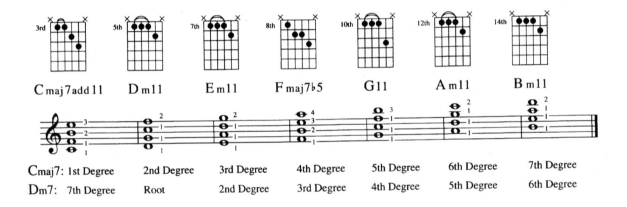

Four-Note Voicings on the Lower Four Strings:

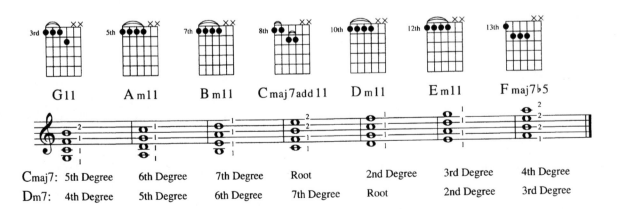

THE SEVEN FUNCTIONS

- One of the most used applications of quartal harmony is on minor 7th chords.

- We can view all of the chordal structures of C Major in relation to the Dm7 chord (iim7).

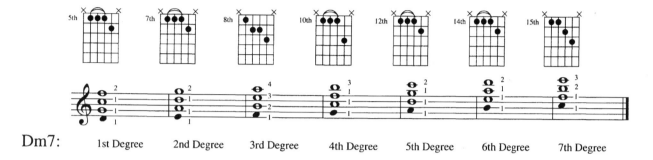

Dm7:   1st Degree   2nd Degree   3rd Degree   4th Degree   5th Degree   6th Degree   7th Degree

Analysis of the Seven Functions:

- If we examine each degree in relation to Dm7, we find the following notes contained in each structure:

1st Degree Structure (or Function):

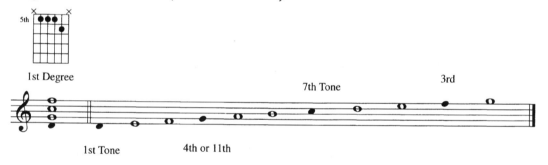

- The notes in the **1st structure** give us the **root**, **4th** (or 11th), **7th**, and **3rd** tones of the Dm chord. Therefore the **1st degree** chord can **function** as Dm with a **7th** and **11th**.

2nd Degree Structure (or Function):

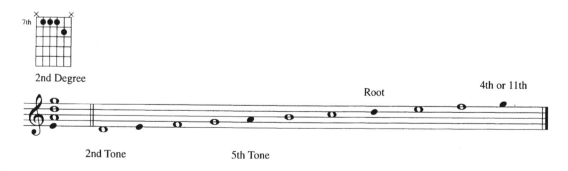

- The **2nd degree** contains the **root** of Dm, the **9th** (or 2nd), the **4th** (or 11th) and **5th**. Therefore the **2nd degree** chord can **function** as Dm with a **9th** and **11th**.

3rd Degree Structure:

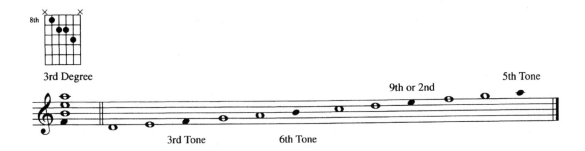

- The **3rd degree** structure contains the **3rd, 6th, 9th** and **5th** of Dm7.
  Therefore the **3rd degree** chord can **function** as Dm with a **13th** (or 6th) and a **9th**.

4th Degree Structure:

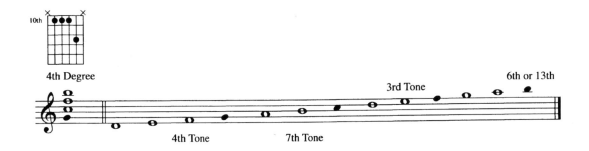

- The **4th degree** structure contains the **4th, 7th, 3rd** and **6th** of Dm7.
  Therefore the **4th degree** chord can **function** as Dm with a an **11th** (or 4th) and **13th** (or 6th)

5th Degree Structure:

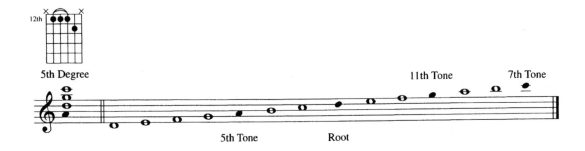

- The **5th degree** contains the **5th, root, 4th** and **7th** of Dm7.
  Therefore the **5th degree** chord can **function** as Dm with an **11th** (or4th) and a **7th**.

6th Degree Structure:

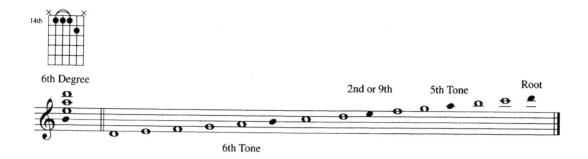

- The **6th degree** structure contains the **6th**, **9th**, **5th** and **root** of Dm7.
  Therefore the **6th degree** chord can **function** as Dm with a **13th** (or 6th) and a **9th**.

7th Degree Structure:

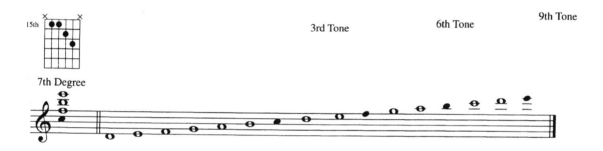

- The **7th degree** structure contains the **7th**, **3rd**, **6th** and **9th** tones of Dm7.
  Therefore the **7th degree** chord can **function** as Dm with a **7th**, a **13th** (or 6th) and a **9th**.

ANALYSIS CHART - 7 STRUCTURES

- If you are creating stuctures in the key of C, starting on C, C would be the 1st degree, D would be the 2nd degree etc.

- If you are creating structures in the key of C starting from D (D - Dorian or Dm7), D would be the 1st degree, E would be the 2nd degree etc.

- The chart below shows the relationship of all seven structures (of D Dorian) to the Dm7 chord

Tone Numbers

	1st	2nd	3rd	4th	5th	6th	7th	8th	9th
D-1st Degree	R		3	4			7		
E-2nd Degree	R	2		4	5				(9)*
F-3rd Degree		2	3		5	6			(9)
G-4th Degree			3	4		6	7		
A-5th Degree	R			4	5		7		
B-6th Degree	R	2			5	6			(9)
C-7th Degree		2	3			6	7		(9)

(left axis label: Structures)

*Note: The 2nd can also be considered the 9th

- **Observation**: When quartal harmonies are created, every structure on every degree contains either the 1st, 3rd, 5th and 7th of Dm.

- **Observation**: Any one of the **7 structures**, created by **harmonizing** the scale in 4ths, can **function** as some sort of Dm chord or **inversion** of Dm7.

- **Conclusion**: – Any scale can be **harmonized** in 4ths (our examples: C Major)
  - The chords created can be named in **traditional** fashion.
  - The chords can also be viewed in a quartal context. In this case, they are referred to as **structures**, and **function** as chords containing 6th, 7ths, 9ths and 3rds.
  - In quartal harmony, the **structures** are identified by **scale degree**: 1st degree structure, 2nd degree structure, etc.

STRUCTURE EXERCISES

- The following exercises are designed to be played over Dm7 (iim7 of C Major).

- All of the structures created in C major can be used as harmonies or functions, played in place of Dm7.

Example 1

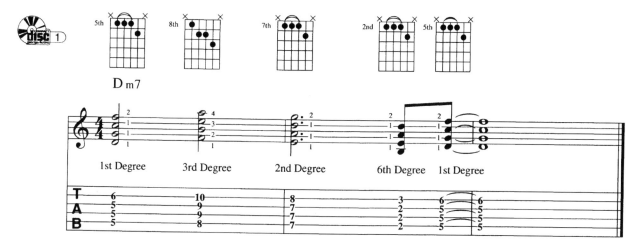

Example 2

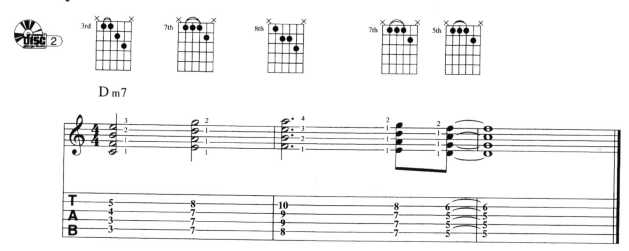

Example 3

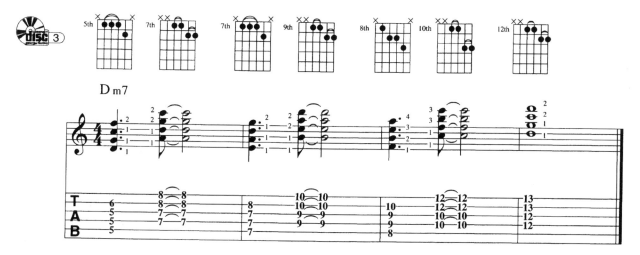

Example 4

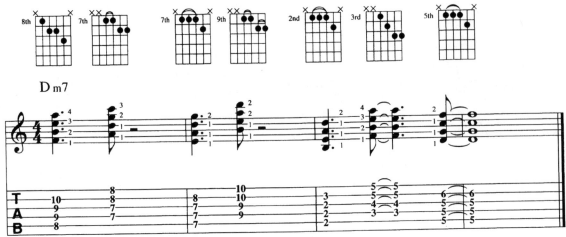

Example 5

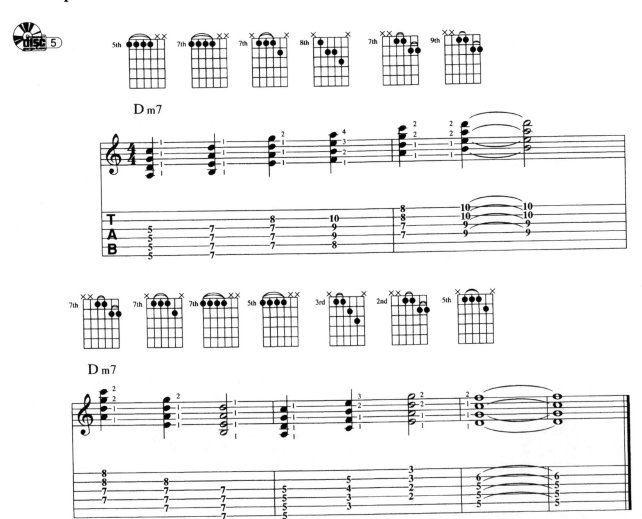

14

Example 6

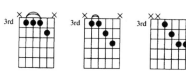
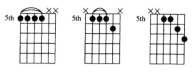

D m7

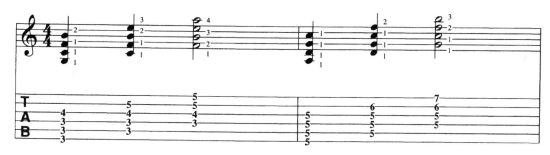

D m7

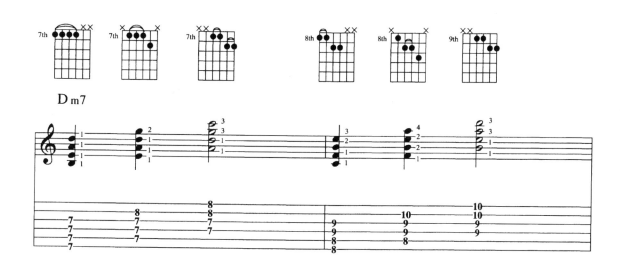

D m7

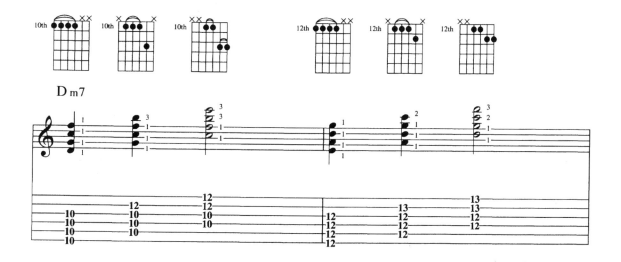

15

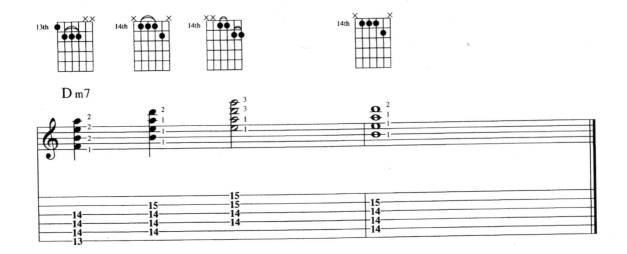

D m7

Example 7

D m7

D m7

EXPANDING QUARTAL STRUCTURES

- We can **expand** our **basic four-note structures** to **five-note structures**.

- Any note from the **tonality** that generates a **four-note structure** can be added to create a **five-note structure**.

- For example, in the key of C major the notes: D-E-F-G-A-B-C can be added to any of the **four-note structures**.

- The tonality of the key of C Major would be: all natural notes (no sharps or flats).

- The added notes can be used to create moving melodic lines.

Example 1

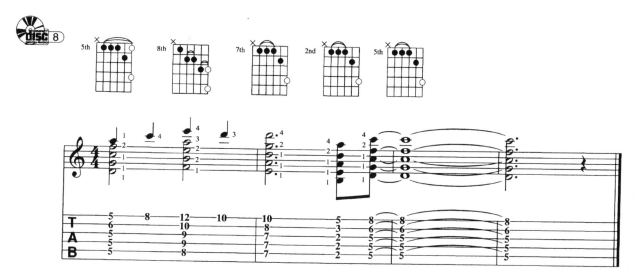

Example 2

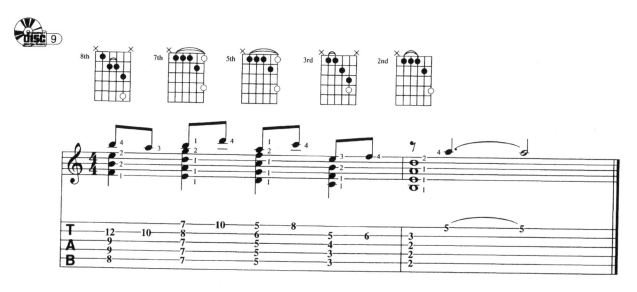

17

Example 3

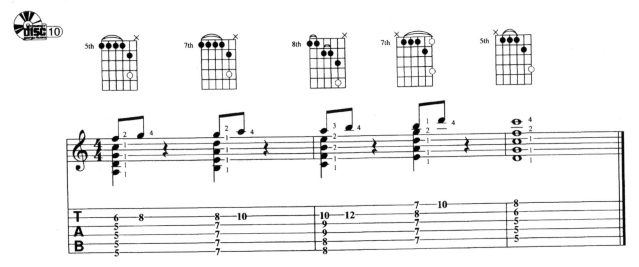

Example 4

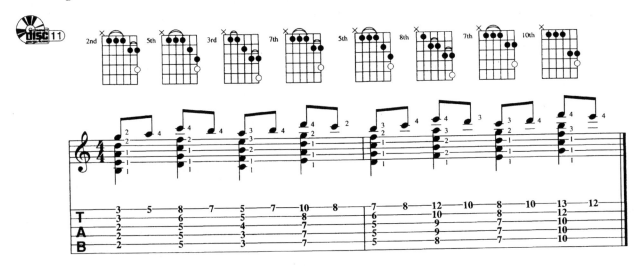

Example 5

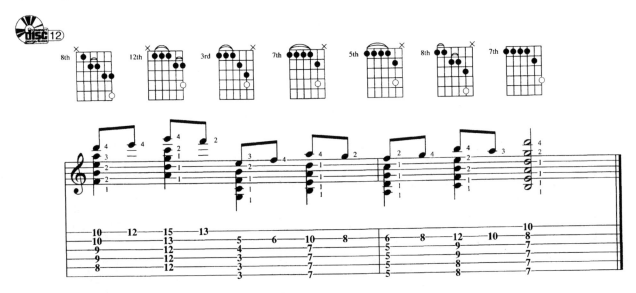

• The next set of examples demonstrates the use of **expanded voicings** used as traditional chords.

Example 1

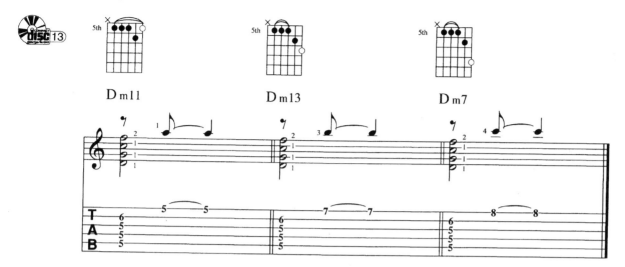

Example 2

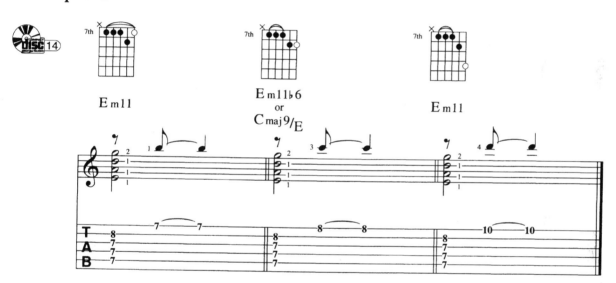

Example 3

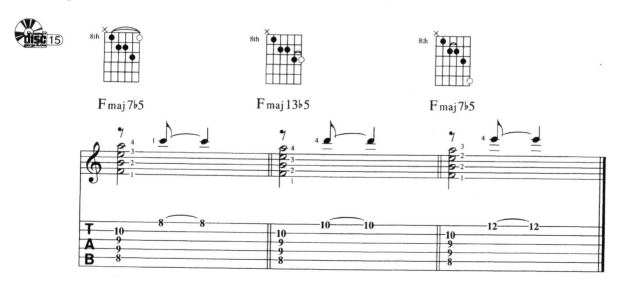

Example 4

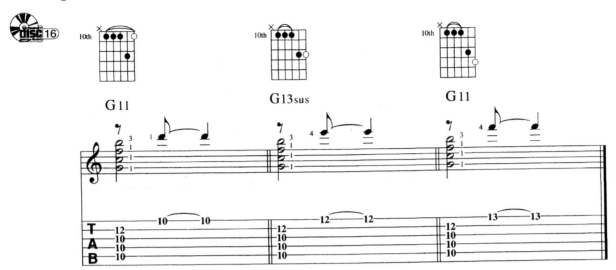

Example 5

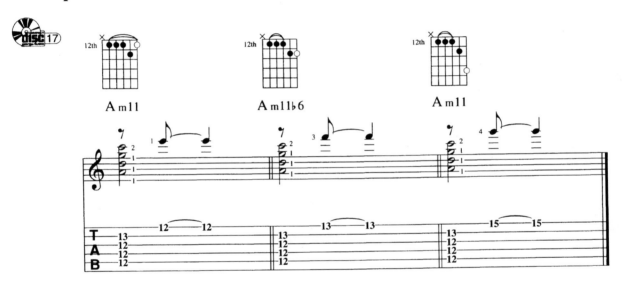

Example 6

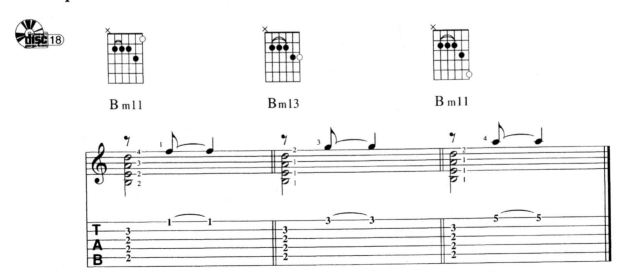

Example 7

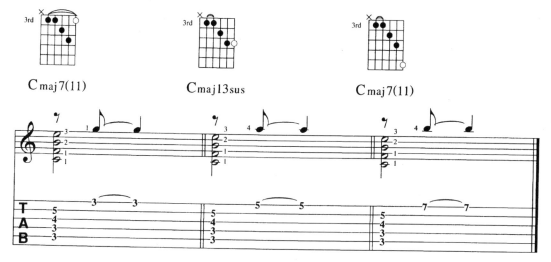

Cmaj7(11)   Cmaj13sus   Cmaj7(11)

QUARTAL STRUCTURES AND TRADITIONAL HARMONY

- As discussed earlier, in traditional harmony, **a major scale generates seven chords**: maj7 - m7 - m7 - maj7 - 7th - m7 - m7♭5

- Quartal structures in the key of C major can be used to produce different sounds for the seven chords of the C major harmonized scale.

- The quartal structures will produce chords containing 7ths, 9ths, 11ths and 13ths.

- The quartal structures can also be used to create **inversions** (voicings starting on the root, 3rd, 5th and 7th of a chord) of the seven harmonized scale chords.

Stylistic Devices: The following examples show how to use 4th harmonies in three very common jazz situations.

1. **Comping Style**: This is another term used for accompaniment. The examples could be used to "comp," while another musician is soloing.
2. **Chord Solo Style**: This style uses chords as harmonies played with the melody of a tune. Both single notes and chords can be used to state the melody being played (similar to a pianist).
3. **Single Notes Leading Into a Structure**: This style uses chords as part of an improvised melodic line.

Cmaj7

- If the 1st, 3rd, 5th and 7th degree structures were played with a C bass note, they would all produce a C Major sounding chord, but the 1st and 3rd degree would be the strongest.

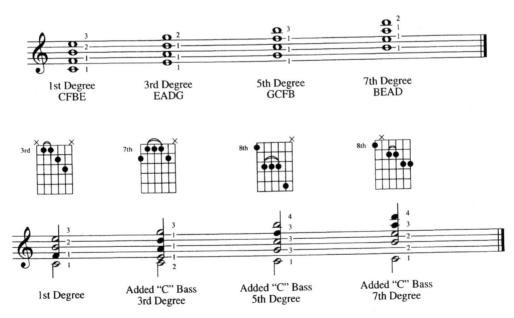

| 1st Degree | 3rd Degree | 5th Degree | 7th Degree |
| CFBE | EADG | GCFB | BEAD |

1st Degree • Added "C" Bass 3rd Degree • Added "C" Bass 5th Degree • Added "C" Bass 7th Degree

- The 1st degree would sound like Cmaj7(11):
  (C) C-F-B-E = 1-11-7-3

- The 3rd degree would sound like C6(9):
  (C) E-A-D-G = 3-6-9-5

- The 5th degree would sound like Cmaj7(add 11):
  (C) G-C-F-B = 5-1-11-7

- The 7th degree would sound like Cmaj13(add 9):
  (C) B-E-A-D = 7-3-13-9

Example 1 - Comping Style: Cmaj7

Example 2 - Chord-Solo Style: Cmaj7

Example 3 - Single Notes Leading Into A Structure: Cmaj7

Dm7 - ii of C major

- If you take the C major scale, starting from the 2nd tone (D), you generate the **D Dorian mode**.

- The 4th structure in C major, starting from the D (2nd tone) creates the Dorian 4th structure.

Dm7

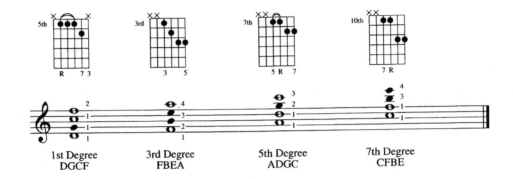

| 1st Degree | 3rd Degree | 5th Degree | 7th Degree |
| DGCF | FBEA | ADGC | CFBE |

- If the above four chords were played with a D bass note, the following voicings would be created:

  - The 1st degree would sound like Dm11
    D-G-C-F = 1-11-♭7-♭3

  - The 3rd degree would sound like Dm13
    (D) F-B-E-A = ♭3-13-9-5

  - The 5th degree would sound like Dm11
    (D) A-D-G-C = 5-1-11-♭7

  - The 7th degree would sound like Dm6(9)
    (D) C-F-B-E = ♭7-♭3-6-9

Example 1 - Comping Style: Dm7

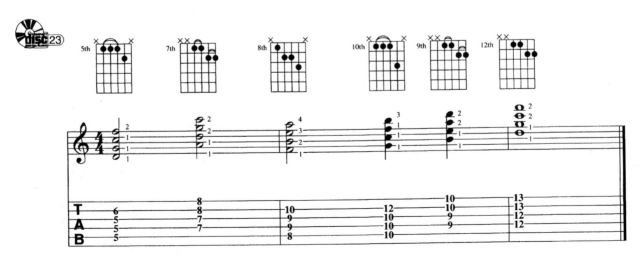

Example 2 - Chord Solo Style: Dm7 (ii of C major)

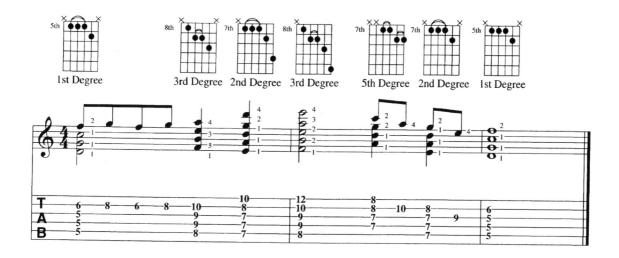

Example 3 - Single Notes Moving Into a Structure: Dm7

- In this example, Dm7 is functioning as the ii chord of C major.

- The notes used to create the solo line are from the key of C major.

- The improvised line is developed around the notes in the Dm7 arpeggio (D-F-A-C).

Em7 - iii of C major

- If you take the C major scale, starting from the 3rd tone (E), you generate the **E Phrygian mode**.

- The 4th structures in C major, starting from E (the 3rd), create the Phrygian 4th structures.

- Some jazz tunes may use Phrygian harmonies indicated by: Em7 (Phrygian).

- The fingerings for the following examples are the same as the fingerings for the C major 4th structures (introduced earlier) starting on the 3rd degree (E).

Em7

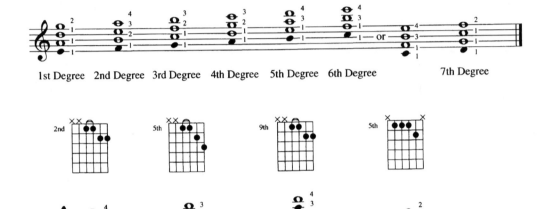

| 1st Degree | 2nd Degree | 3rd Degree | 4th Degree | 5th Degree | 6th Degree | 7th Degree |

| 1st Degree | 3rd Degree | 5th Degree | 7th Degree |
| EADG | GCFB | BCAD | DGCF |

- The 1st degree: **E-A-D-G = 1-11-♭7-♭3** = Em11

- The 3rd degree: **G-C-F-B** = ♭3-♭6-♭9-5 = Em

- The 5th degree: **B-C-A-D** = 5-♭6-11-♭7 = Em11(♭6)

- The 7th degree: **D-G-C-F** = ♭7-♭3-♭6-♭9 = Em

Example 1 - Comping Style: Em7

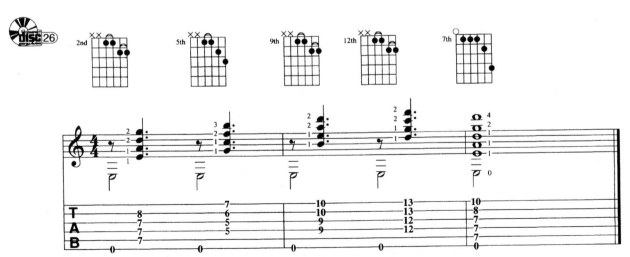

Example 2 - Chord-Solo Style: Em7 - (iii of C major)

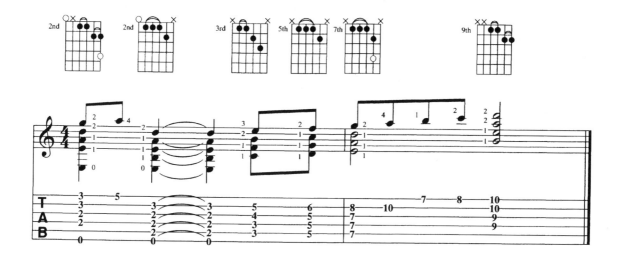

Example 3 - Single Notes Moving Into a Structure: Em7

- The improvised line is created by using the key of C major guided by the arpeggio of the Em7 chord (E-G-B-D).

- In this example (and all examples in this section) the chord is functioning as one of the chords in C major.

- Em7 is the iii chord of C major.

- Em7 is also the 1st chord of E Phrygian.

Fmaj7 - IV of C major

- If you take the C major scale, starting from the 4th tone "F", you generate the **F Lydian mode**.

- The 4th structures in C major starting from the F (4th tone) create the Lydian 4th structure.

Fmaj7

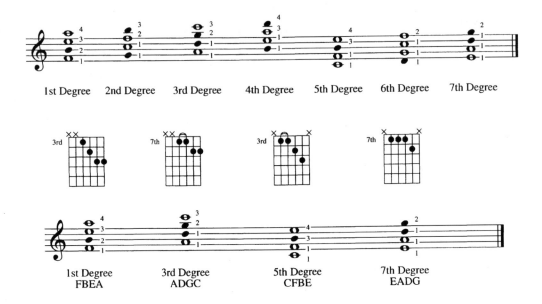

- The 1st degree: **F-B-E-A = 1-#11-7-3** = Fmaj7#11

- The 3rd degree: **A-D-G-C = 3-6-9-5** = Fmaj6(9)

- The 5th degree: **C-F-B-E = 5-1-#11-7** = Fadd9 (#11)

- The 7th degree: **E-A-D-G = 7-3-6-9** = Fmaj6(9)

Example 1 - Comping Style: Fmaj7

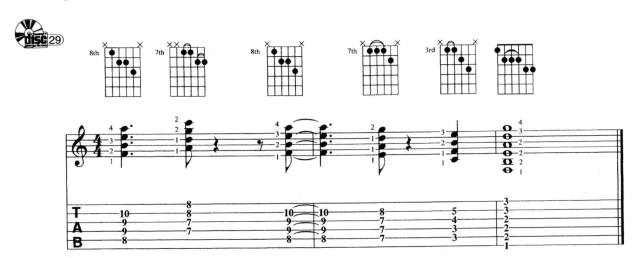

Example 2 - Chord Solo Style: Fmaj7 (IV of C major)

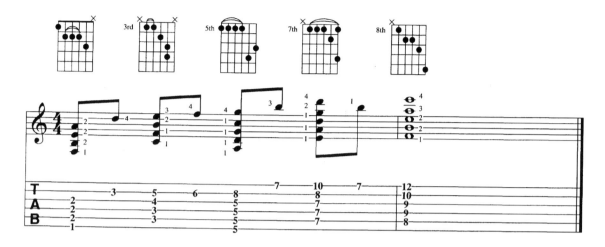

Example 3 - Single Notes Moving Into A Structure: Fmaj7

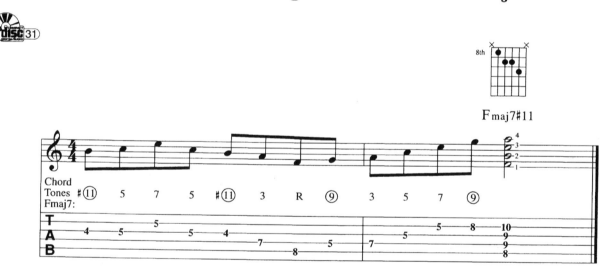

Fmaj7#11

G7 - V of C major

- If you take the C major scale, starting from the 5th tone (G), you generate the **G Mixolydian mode**.

- The 4th structure in C major starting from the G (5th tone) creates the Mixolydian 4th srructures.

G7

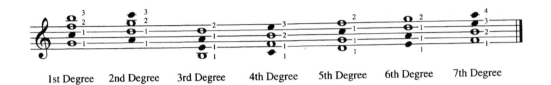

| 1st Degree | 2nd Degree | 3rd Degree | 4th Degree | 5th Degree | 6th Degree | 7th Degree |

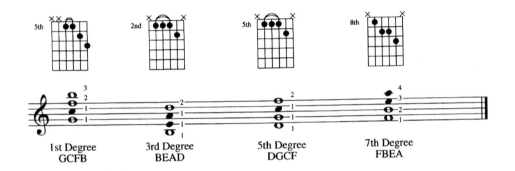

| 1st Degree | 3rd Degree | 5th Degree | 7th Degree |
| GCFB | BEAD | DGCF | FBEA |

- The 1st degree: **G-C-F-B = 1-11-♭7-3** =G(11)

- The 3rd degree: **B-E-A-D = 3-13-9-5** = G(13)

- The 5th degree: **D-G-C-F = 5-1-11-♭7** = G(13sus)

- The 7th degree: **F-B-E-A** = ♭7-3-13-9 = G(13)

Example 1 - Comping Style: G7

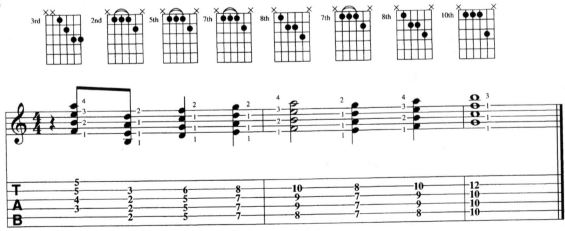

Example 2 - Chord Solo Style: G7 (V of C major)

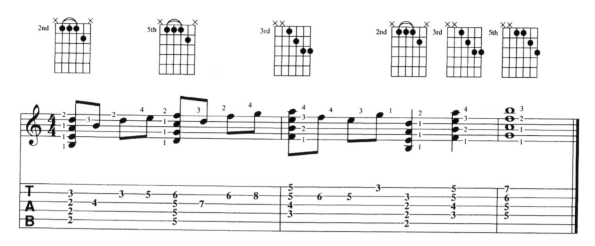

Example 3 - Single Notes Leading Into a Structure: G7

Am7 - vi of C major

- If you take the C major scale starting from the 6th tone (A), you generate the **A Aeolian mode**.

- The 4th structures in the key of C major starting from A (the 6th tone) create the Aeolian 4th structures.

Am7

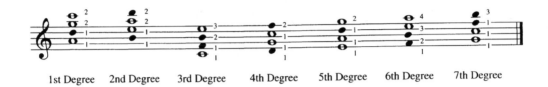

| 1st Degree | 2nd Degree | 3rd Degree | 4th Degree | 5th Degree | 6th Degree | 7th Degree |

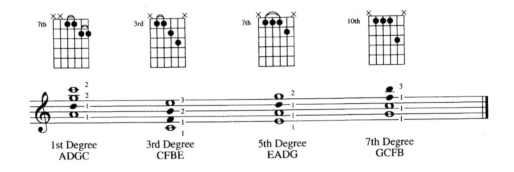

| 1st Degree | 3rd Degree | 5th Degree | 7th Degree |
| ADGC | CFBE | EADG | GCFB |

- The 1st degree: **A-D-G-C** = **1-4-7-3** = Am(11)

- The 3rd degree: **C-F-B-E** = **3-♭6-9-5** = Am9(♭6)

- The 5th degree: **E-A-D-G** = **5-1-11-7** = Am(11)

- The 7th degree: **G-C-F-B** = **7-3-♭6-9** = Am9(♭6)

Example 1 - Comping Style: Am7

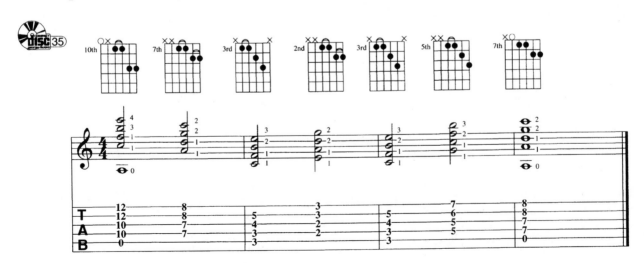

Example 2 - Chord Solo Style: Am7 (vi of C major)

Example 3 - Single Notes Leading Into a Structure: Am7

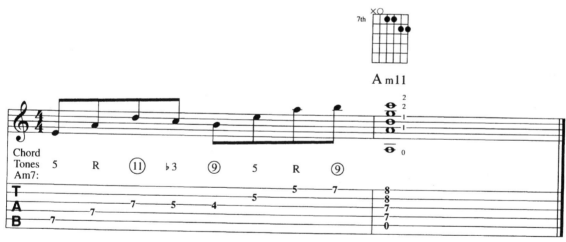

Bm7♭5 - vii of C major

- If you take the C major scale starting from the 7th tone (B), you generate the **B Locrian mode**.

- The 4th structures in the key of C major starting from B (the 7th tone) create the Locrian 4th structures.

Bm7♭5

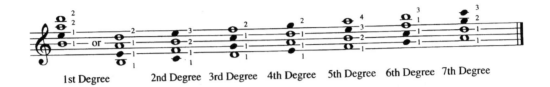

1st Degree   2nd Degree   3rd Degree   4th Degree   5th Degree   6th Degree   7th Degree

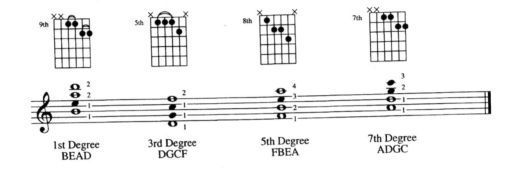

1st Degree
BEAD

3rd Degree
DGCF

5th Degree
FBEA

7th Degree
ADGC

- The 1st degree: **B-E-A-D** = **1-11-♭7-♭3** = Bm(11)

- The 3rd degree: **D-G-C-F** = ♭3-♭6-♭9-♭5 = Bm9(♭6,♭9)

- The 5th degree: **F-B-E-A** = ♭5-1-11-♭7 = Bm (11,♭5)

- The 7th degree: **A-D-G-C** = ♭7-♭3-♭6-♭9 = Bm9 (♭6,♭6)

Example 1 - Comping Style: Bm7♭5

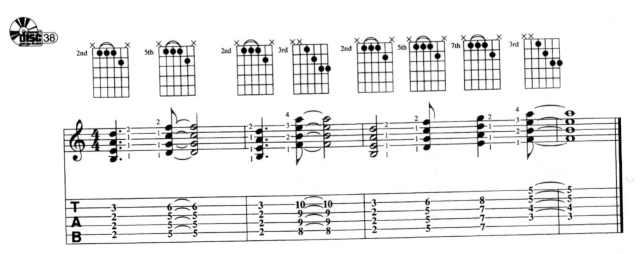

Example 2 - Chord Solo Style: Bm7♭5 (vii of C major)

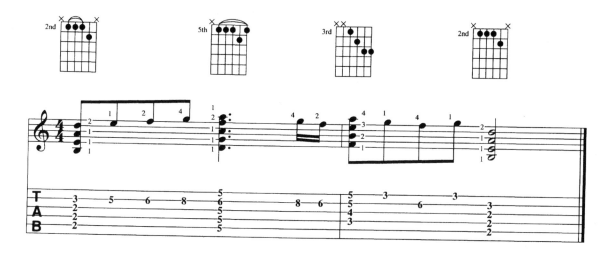

Example 3 - Single Notes Leading Into a Structure: Bm7♭5

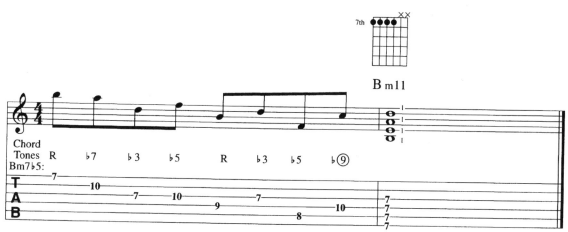

CREATING OUTSIDE SOUNDS

The simplest explanation of outside comping or soloing would be: using notes of a scale or chord that do not belong to the same key as the chord being played.

Charlie Parker and John Coltrane developed almost every concept of "inside" and "outside" playing in use today.

Charlie Parker developed substitutions in related keys a minor 3rd apart. Parker's concept is sometimes referred to as "The Parker Cycle."

John Coltrane developed substitutions in related keys a major 3rd apart. His concept is referred to as "The Coltrane Cycle" or "The Giant Step Cycle."

Minor 3rd Substitution

• For Dm7 (iim7 chord of C), we can substitute Fm7 (iim7 of Eb), Abm7 (iim7 of Gb), and Bm7 (iim7 of A).

• The fingerings are shown below on the inside 4 strings.

Substitute Fm7: (ii of Eb) shapes for Dm7

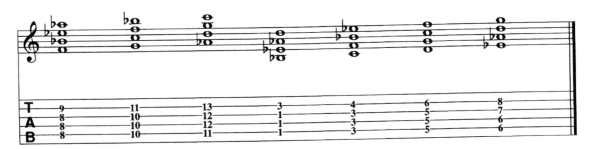

Substitute Abm7: (ii of Gb) shapes for Dm7

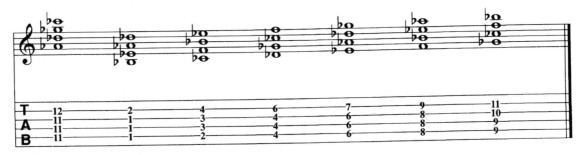

Substitute Bm7: (ii of A) shapes for Dm7

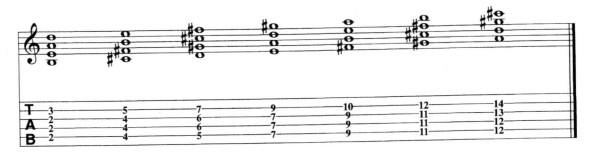

The following chart shows the minor 3rd relationship from all 12 possibilities.

C	E♭	G♭	A
F	A♭	C♭	D
B♭	D♭	F♭	G
E♭	G♭	B♭♭	C
A♭	C♭	E♭♭	F
D♭	F♭	A♭♭	B♭
G♭	B♭♭	D♭♭	E♭
B	D	F	A♭
E	G	B♭	D♭
A	C	E♭	G♭/F♯
D	F	A♭	B
G	B♭	D♭	E

• The four related keys starting from Cm7 would be: Cm - E♭m - G♭m - Am.

• The four related keys starting from Dm would be: Dm - Fm - A♭m - Bm.

The 1st minor 3rd substitute is Dm7 - Fm7

Example 1 - Dm7 to Fm7

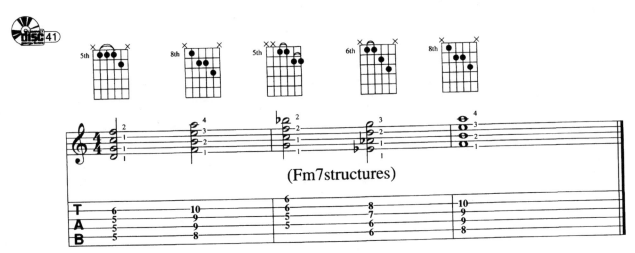

(Fm7structures)

- The above exercise started on Dm7 (iim7 of C) then went "outside" to Fm7 (iim7 of E♭), then came back to Dm7 (iim7 of C).

- This device is sometimes called "side slipping."

Example 2 - Dm7 to Fm7

Tune the sixth string (E) to (D) - to hear the "outside relationship" better.

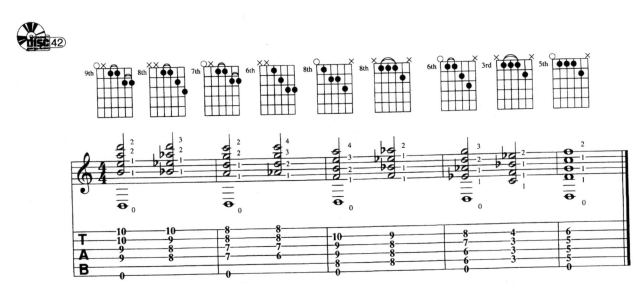

Example 3 - Dm7 to Fm7

Tune the sixth string (E) to D

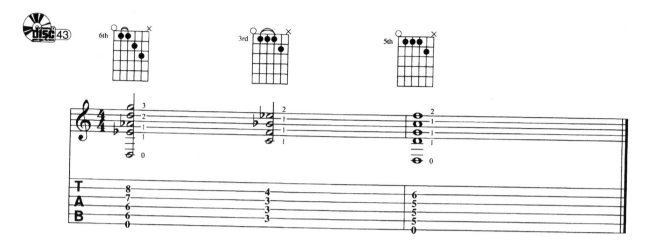

The next minor 3rd substitute is Dm7 - A♭m7

- Notice that the "A♭" is the ♭5th of D.

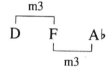

$$D \quad F \quad A♭$$

- This is sometimes referred to as the ♭5 substitute or the "tri-tone" substitute.

Example 4 - Dm7 to A♭m7

Tune the sixth string (E) to D

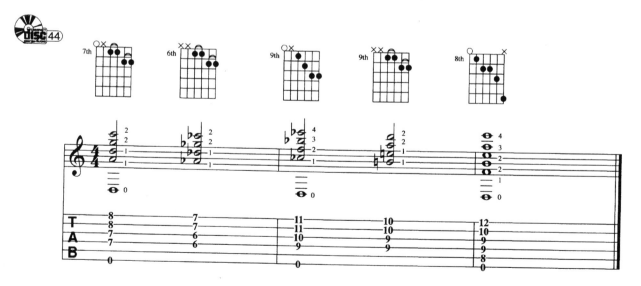

Example 5 - Dm7 to A♭m7

Tune the sixth string (E) to D

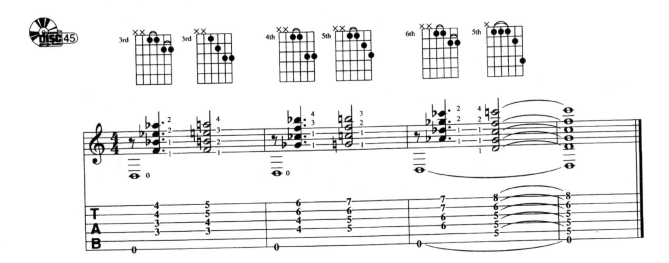

The next minor 3rd substitute is Dm7 - Bm7

• The farther you move away from the tonic key; the functions become more "outside".

Example 6 - Dm7 to Bm7

Tune the sixth string (E) to D

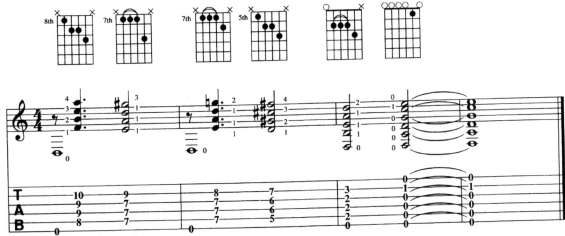

Major 3rd Substitution

• The next set of examples, deal with substitutions in major 3rds.

• For example, starting on D - F# - A#

• It is recommended to study the solos and analysis of John Coltrane in this area.

• The following chart shows the major 3rd relationship for all 12 possibilities.

C	E	G#
F	A	C#
Bb	D	F#
Eb	G	B
Ab	C	E
Db	F	A
Gb	Bb	D
B	D#	Fx
E	G#	B#
A	C#	E#
D	F#	A#
G	B	D#

Example 1 - Dm7 (iim7 of C major) moving up a major 3rd to F#m7 (iim7 of Emajor)

Tune the sixth string (E) to D

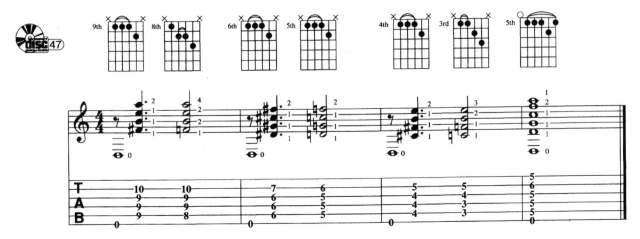

Example 2 - Dm7 moving up to F#m7

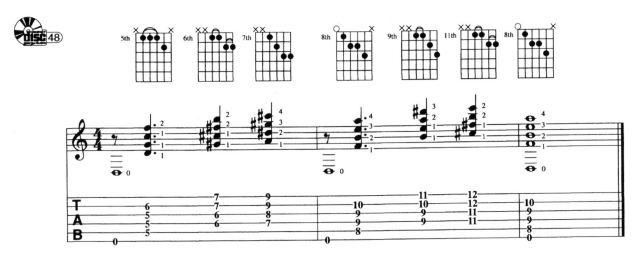

Example 3 - Dm7 moving up to A#m7, in this case B♭m7 (iim7 of A♭)

Tune the sixth string (E) to D

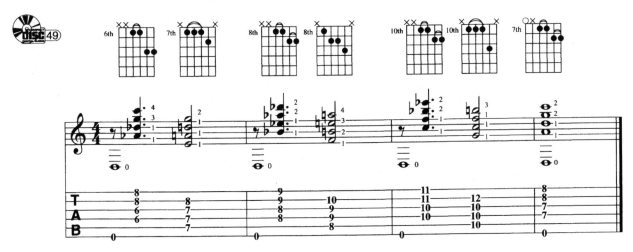

Example 4 - Dm7 to B♭m7

Tune the sixth string (E) to D

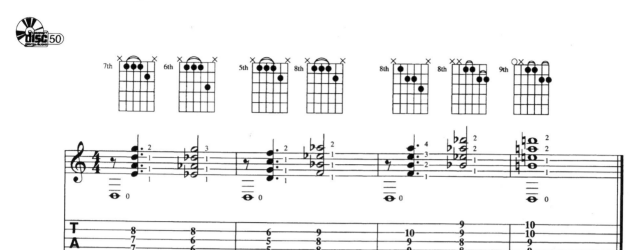

Combinining the 3 related keys:

Example 5 - Dm7, F#m7, B♭m7 (or A#m7)

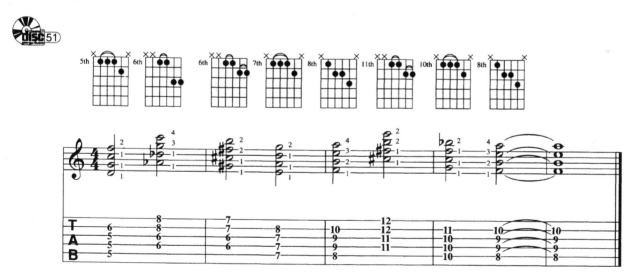

CHROMATIC MOVEMENT

- A structure (or function) $\frac{1}{2}$ step above or below another structure can be used as a "leading" structure.

- The leading structure resolves to a "target" structure.

Example

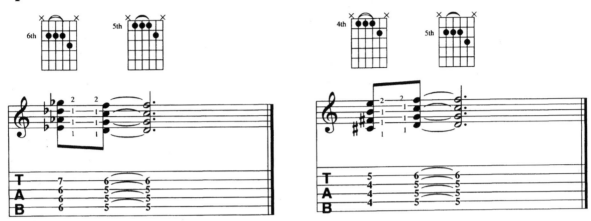

- The following examples use chromatic movement to target different functions in the key of C major.

- Expanded voicings are also used.

- The following examples could be applied in tunes like "Impressions" by John Coltrane or "So What" by Miles Davis.

Example 1

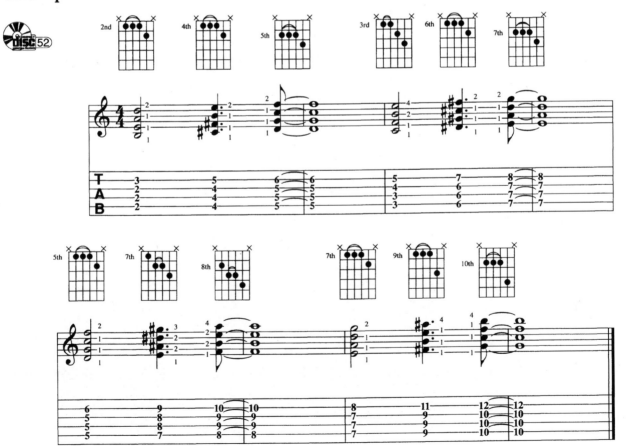

Example 2

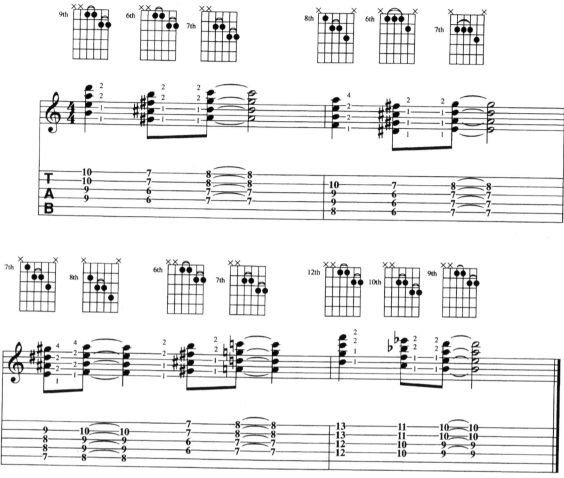

Example 3

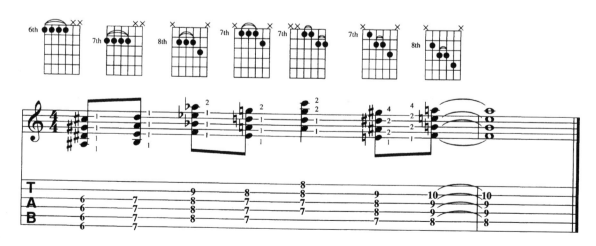

Example 4

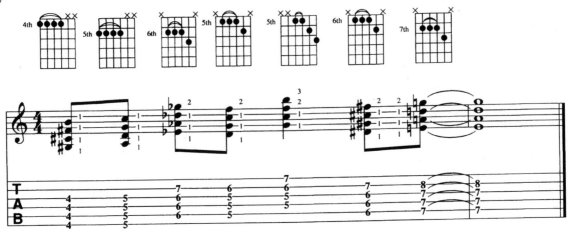

Example 5

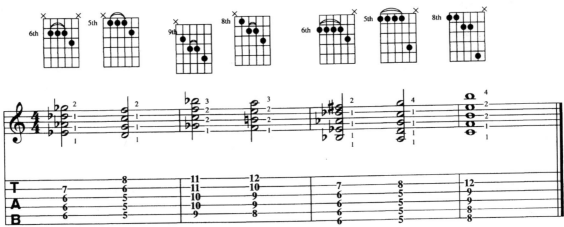

CONTRARY MOTION

- Contrary Motion is when you have lines moving up and down at the same time.

- We can create this type of movement in quartal harmony by taking a structure, move the highest tone up ½ step and the lower 3 tones down ½ step. Then, resolve all the tones to the original tructure.

Example

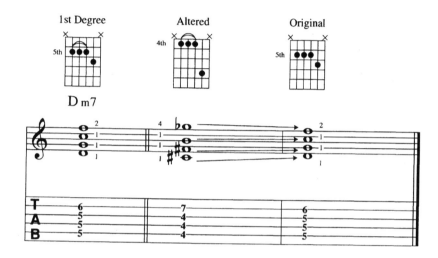

Example 1

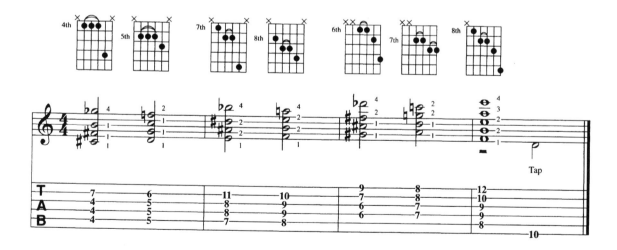

47

Example 2

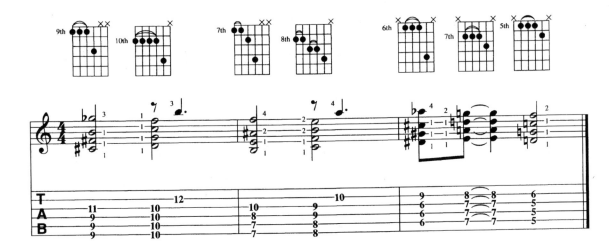

Example 3

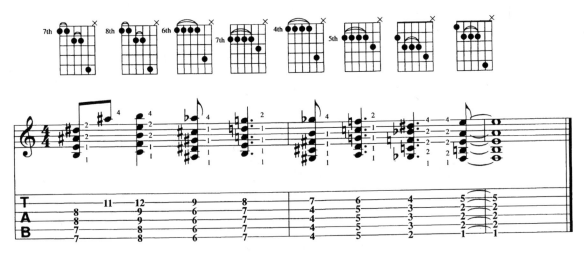

CONTRARY MOTION WITH ADDED BASS NOTE

- The 4th structures can be multiplied to endless possibilities by adding bass notes.

- Any of the twelve chromatic tones can be added to any structure.

- Voice leading concepts are also applied in the following exercises:

Example 1

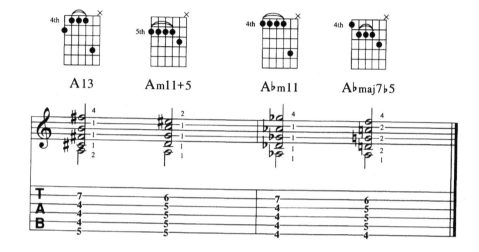

A13   Am11+5   Abm11   Abmaj7b5

- Many chords created, using the concepts above, can be used to compose chord movements that depart from the traditional ii -V - I.

- Some of these chords contain inner voice movements and upper voice movements in both directions at the same time.

- The movements within the chord changes shown in the example above, (and in the following examples), generate harmonies that depart from traditional chord types.

Example 2

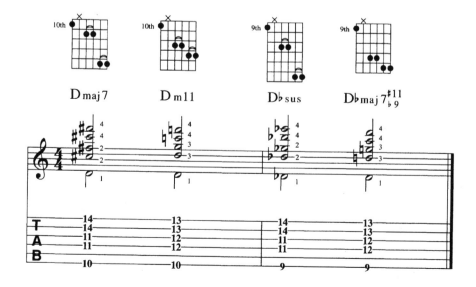

Dmaj7   Dm11   Dbsus   Dbmaj7$^{\sharp 11}_{\flat 9}$

Example 3

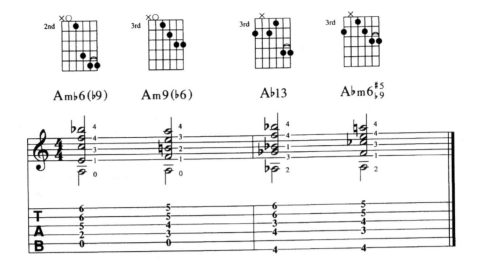

Example 4

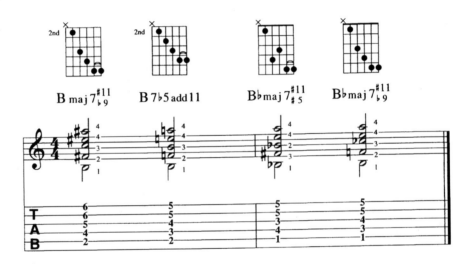

Example 5

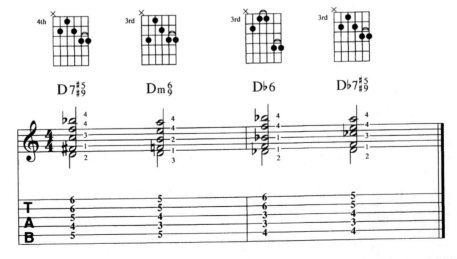

CREATING ii-V-I PROGRESSIONS

Key of C major: ii-V-I = Dm7-G7-Cmaj7

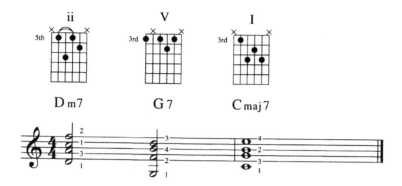

Voice Leading

- Voice leading refers to the movement of each voice (note) to another voice (note).

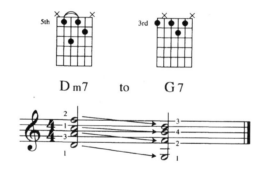

- In order to add more "color" to the progression, most jazz musicians "alter" the V chord. Altering means to add **non-diatonic** notes.

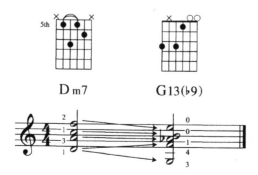

ii - V - I Exercises

- The following examples start on a Dm7 quartal structure. From there, voice leading is used to create an **altered G7**.

- The G7 is then resolved to a Cmaj7 quartal structure.

- Cmaj7 besides being the **I chord** of C major, is also the **IV** chord of G major.

- 4th structures in the key of G major can be used to create Cmaj7 structures with #11ths (F#).

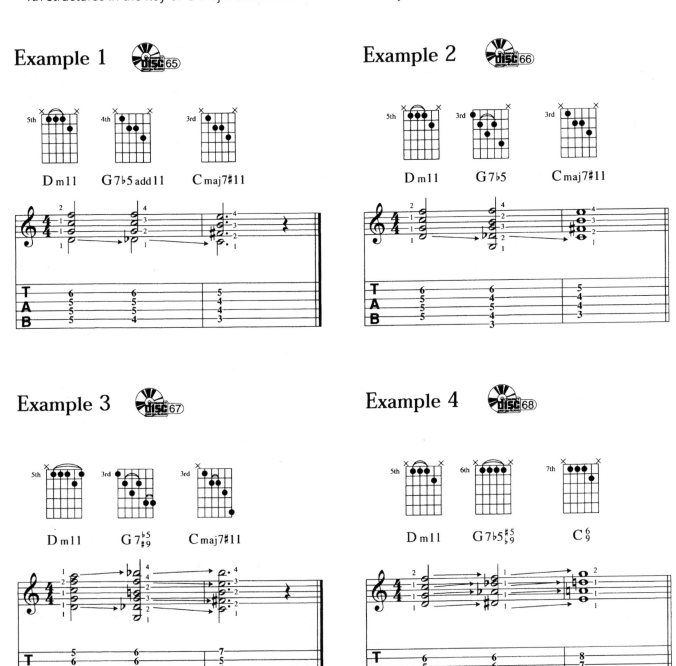

Example 1

Example 2

Example 3

Example 4

Example 5

Example 6

Example 7

Example 8

Example 9

Example 10

53

Example 11
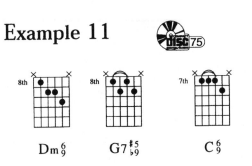

Example 12
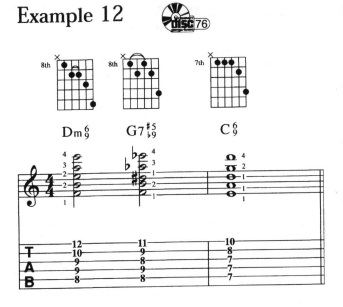

Example 13
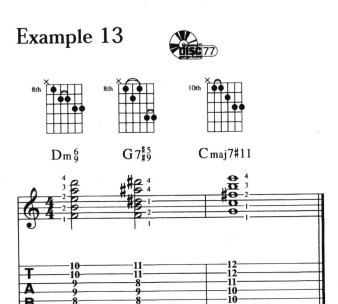

Example 14
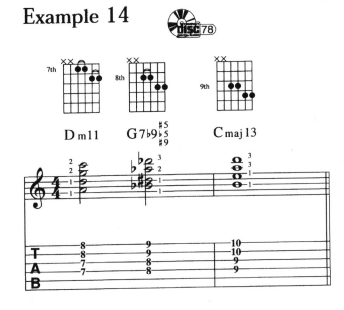

Example 15
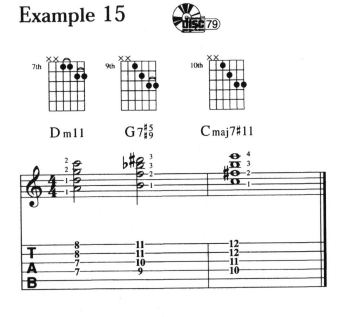

Example 16
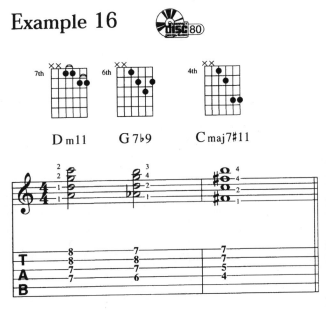

Example 17

Example 18

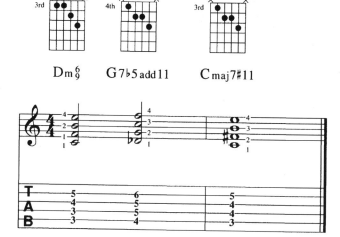

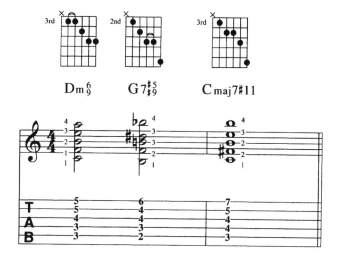

Example 19

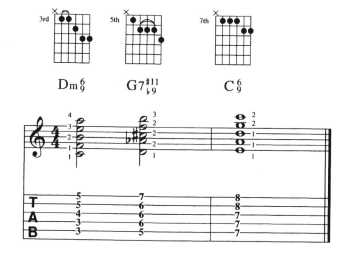

VARIATIONS OF QUARTAL VOICINGS

- The basic 4th structure can be changed to create a voicing more common to keyboard players.

- Take the 1st two notes (of the voicing below D - G), then go up a diatonic step (key of C major) and build a 4th on top of that note (A - D).

Example

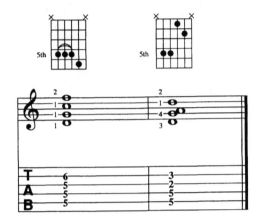

5th and 4th String Forms

- The following fingerings are for the "keyboard type" voicings, starting on the 5th and 4th strings.

- The 6th string forms are not being shown because the voicings tend to get "muddy".

- You can play the top or bottom three notes of any of these chords to create 3-note forms.

5th String Forms:

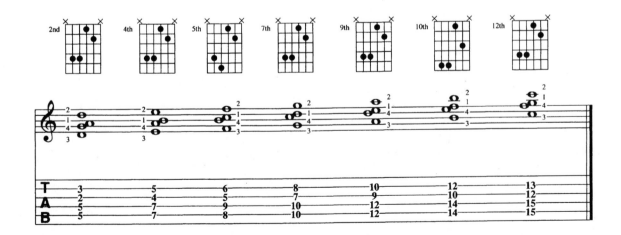

4th String Forms:

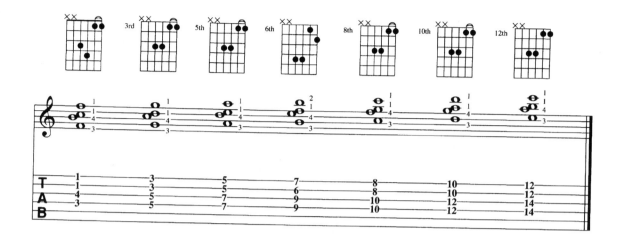

• The voicings shown above will be used in the final section of this book ("Jazz Tunes").

HARMONIC MINOR

- As mentioned earlier, any scale can be harmonized in fourths.

- The harmonic minor is one of the main scales in traditional harmony.

- In the key of A harmonic minor, G notes are sharped. This turns the "V" chord E into an E7 chord.

A - Natural Minor:

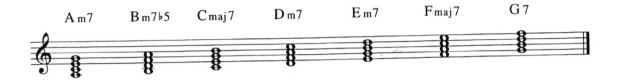

A - Harmonic Minor:

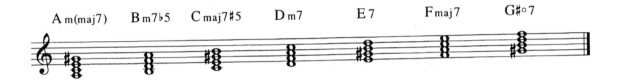

Key of A: Harmonic Minor-Traditional

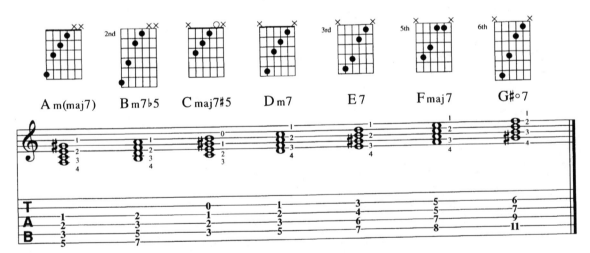

- The harmonic minor scale is very important because it produces chords not found in major harmony.

- Perhaps the most important extract from the harmonic minor, in Jazz, is the **Minor ii - V: Bmi7♭5 to E7♭9** (in A minor).

- **Bmi7♭5 to E7♭9** will be used later in the book in the tune "500 Chicks."

Harmonic Minor Quartal Harmony

• The harmonic minor can be harmonized in 4ths in the same fashion as the major scale.

Key of A: Harmonic Minor

Four-Note Voicings on the Upper Four Strings:

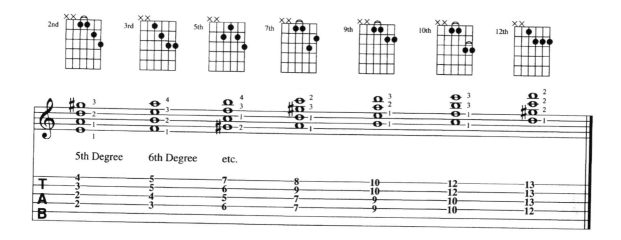

• Note that harmonic minor quartal harmonies create a couple of situations that change the 4th interval.

• The interval G - C is a 4th.

• Once the G is sharped (G♯), **G♯ - C** becomes a **major 3rd interval**.

Four-Note Voicings on the Middle Four Strings:

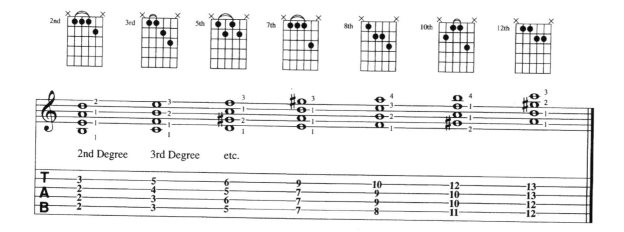

Four-Note Voicings on the Bottom Four Strings:

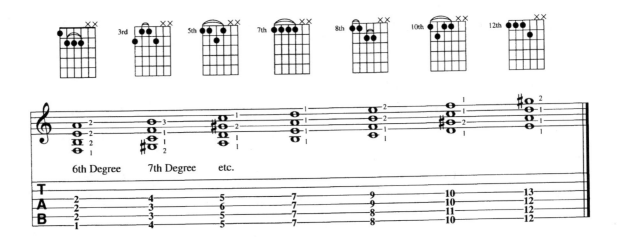

Variations of the Quartal Structures

• The quartal voicings of "A" harmonic minor will now be changed into the "keyboard" type voicings.

• Only the top four and middle four string groups will be used.

Key of A: Harmonic Minor

Four-Note Voicings on the Upper Four Strings:

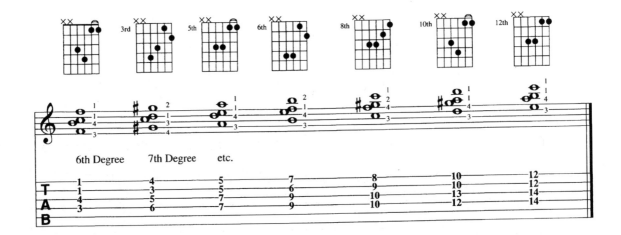

Four-Note Voicings on the Middle Four Strings:

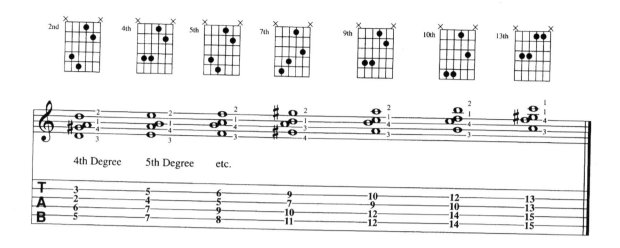

- All of the exercises performed in Dm7 can be moved to "A" harmonic minor.

- This can be done by scale degree.

- **Example**: page 13 example 1, uses 1st degree to 3rd degree to 2nd degree of Dm.

- You could play this same example in "A" harmonic minor - 1st degree to 3rd degree etc.

- You can use the degrees of the scale on any string group.

Example - Dm7 (ii of C Major)

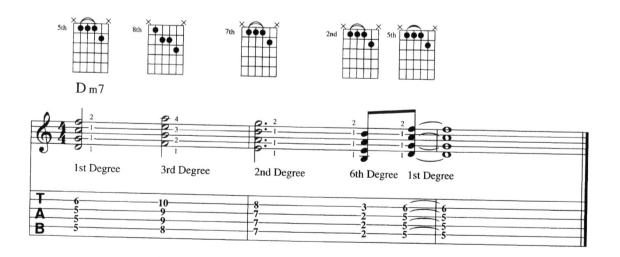

A Harmonic Minor

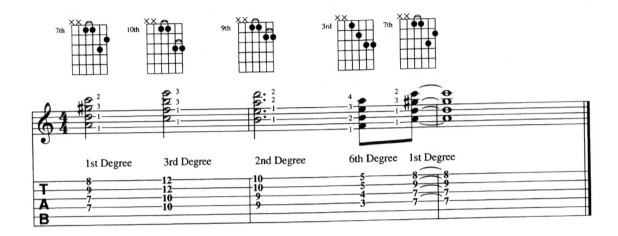

1st Degree   3rd Degree   2nd Degree   6th Degree   1st Degree

MINOR BLUES

• Many tunes written using the **12-bar minor blues** use the following chords:

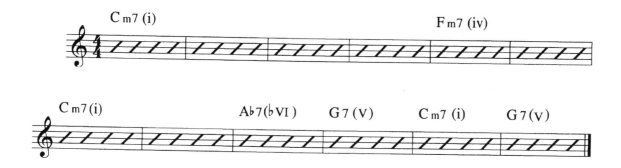

• More changes can be added to the minor blues to create the following progression.

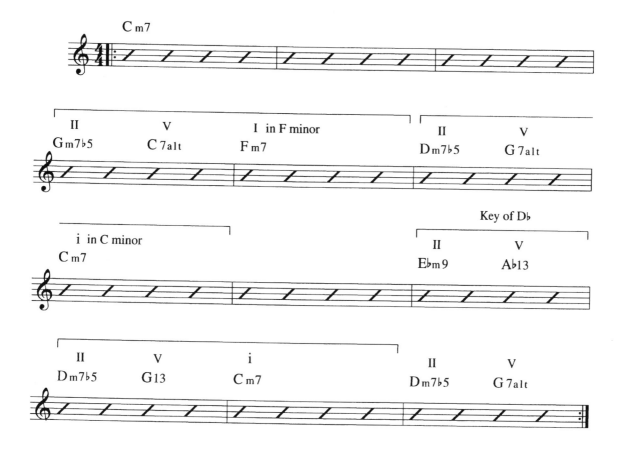

• Now take the minor blues and substitute quartal harmony functions for the traditional chords.

• The traditional chord names are written above the measures.

Minor Blues Quartal Harmony

JAZZ TUNES

The next section contains songs that are based upon chord progressions to many famous jazz compositions.

Miles Davis, Chick Corea, Freddie Hubbard, Wayne Shorter and Herbie Hancock are some of the leading composers of jazz music that lends itself to quartal harmony concepts.

The following examples demonstrate the use of quartal harmonies on tunes that are similar to "500 Miles High," "Footprints," "Blue In Green," "Nefertiti," and "Little Sunflower."

The chord changes, written above each measure, show the kind of chords used in most charts.

"500 CHICKS"

"HAND PRINTS"

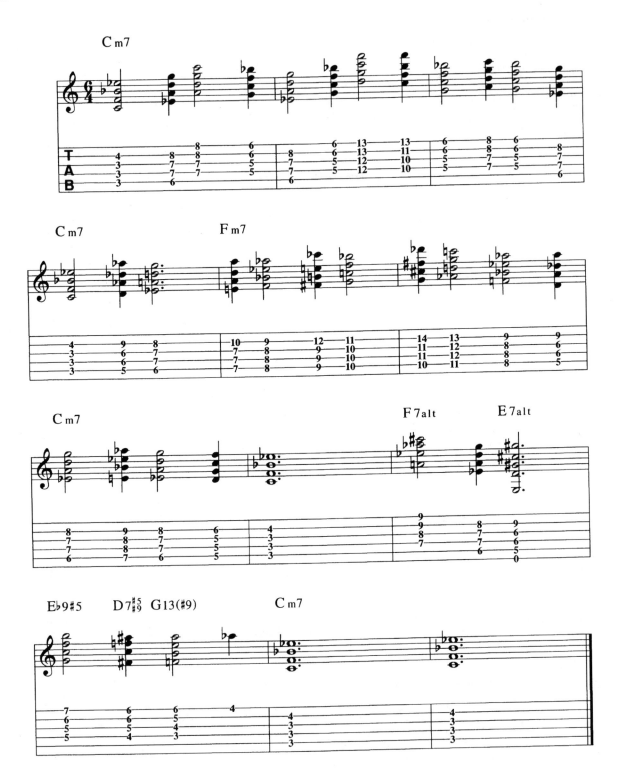

"Black In Grey"

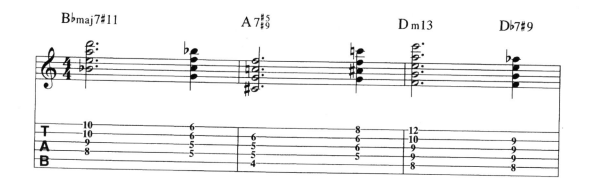

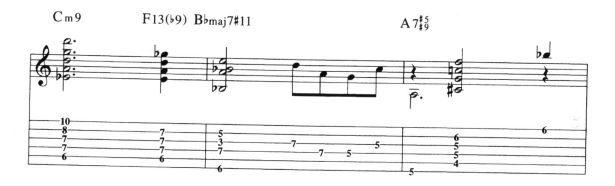

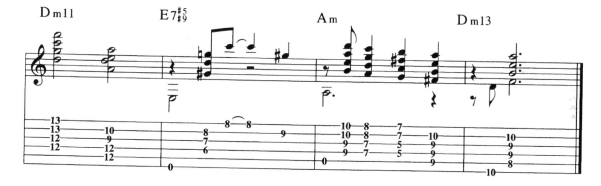

"NEVER TARDY"

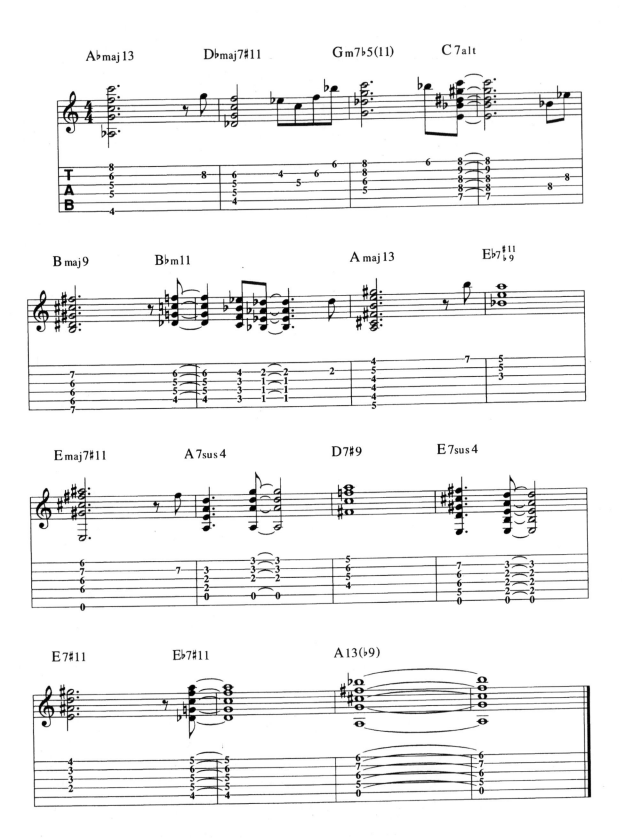

"BIG MOON FLOWER"

Tune sixth string to D

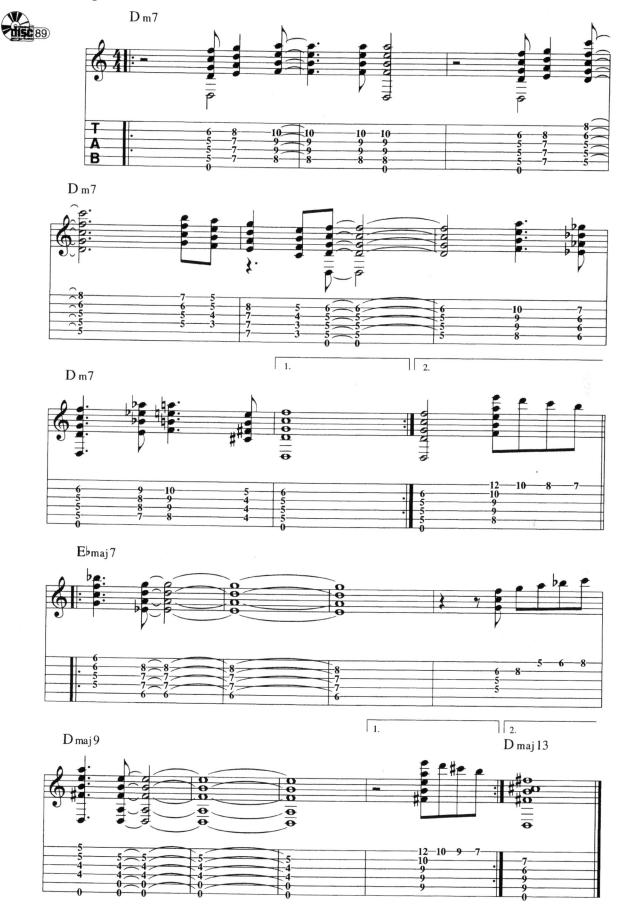

CLOSING NOTES

The use of quartal harmonies created a new freedom of expression in jazz. Freedom of expression and creativity should be a major consideration of a jazz musician.

While writing this book, it was necessary to explain many of the concepts in complete theoretical terms. The explanations are for analytical considerations.

It is not necessary to memorize every analysis contained in this book. Try to get a basic feel for the concepts and let your intuitive sense take over.

Charlie Parker was known for telling musicians to learn everything that they could about music, then to forget it all, and just play. If you are interested in applying chordal harmony concepts, this book could be used as one of the first steps in Parker's philosophy.

I was very fortunate to study with Pat Martino. Two ideas that Pat conveyed to me made a major impact in my approach to music. The first is to contemplate what you want to accomplish, and then figure out a way to do it. The second is, that people only accept new ideas when they are ready to accept them (From the book "I Ching").

I would like to thank Mel Bay Publishing, Inc. for their dedication to musical education and for their support and encouragement in this project. And to the memory of Thomas W. Puckett (12/9/69 - 10/5/02), who did the layout and engraving for this book.

I would like to thank Professor Vince Bredice. He encouraged me to write out all my ideas and concepts. His help and input was the major factor in getting my first manuscript published.

Special thanks to my wife JoAnn, without her help I could have never completed this project.

~ Tom Floyd ~

WWW.MELBAY.COM

Made in the USA
Middletown, DE
19 February 2018